COUNTRY INSIGHTS

KENYA

Máiréad Dunne, Wambui Kairi,
and Eric Nyanjom

RSVP
**RAINTREE
Steck-Vaughn**
P U B L I S H E R S
The Steck-Vaughn Company

Austin, Texas

COUNTRY INSIGHTS

BRAZIL • CHINA • CUBA • CZECH REPUBLIC • DENMARK • INDIA
FRANCE • JAMAICA • JAPAN • KENYA • MEXICO • PAKISTAN

GUIDE TO THIS BOOK

In addition to telling you about the whole of Kenya, this book looks closely at the city of Mombasa and at the village of Matinyani.

 Each time the book discusses Mombasa, this city symbol will appear at the top of the page and information boxes.

 This rural symbol will appear each time the book discusses Matinyani.

Title page: Schoolchildren from Bomu School, in Mombasa, hold up the leaves they are studying in their nature lesson.

Contents page: Mount Kenya (*Kirinyaga*), rising above the clouds in central Kenya

Published by Raintree Steck-Vaughn Publishers, an imprint of Steck-Vaughn Company

Library of Congress Cataloging-in-Publication Data
Dunne, Máiréad; Nyanjom, Eric; and Wambui, Kairi.
Kenya / Máiréad Dunne.
    p.   cm.—(Country Insights)
    Includes bibliographical references and index.
    Summary: Introduces the landscape, climate, culture, and possible future of Kenya.
    ISBN 0-8172-4790-4
    1. Kenya—Juvenile literature.
    [1. Kenya.] I. Kairi, Wambui. II. Nyanjom, Eric.
    III. Title. IV. Series.
    DT433.522.D86   1997
    967.62—dc21   96-52703

Printed in Italy. Bound in the United States.
1 2 3 4 5 6 7 8 9 0 02 01 00 99 98

Contents

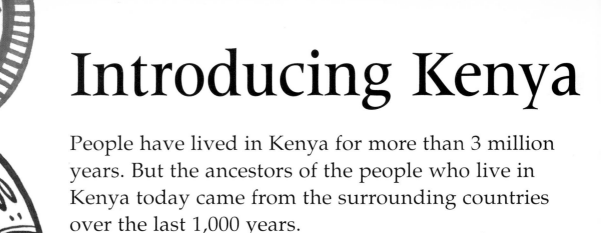

Introducing Kenya

People have lived in Kenya for more than 3 million years. But the ancestors of the people who live in Kenya today came from the surrounding countries over the last 1,000 years.

From A.D. 1500, many traders visited the Kenyan coast for spices and slaves. Eventually, in 1895, British explorers formed a colony. In 1920, Kenya was named after its highest mountain, the snow-capped Mount Kenya, or *Kirinyaga*, which means "Mountain of God."

During the time the British were in charge, many Africans worked on farms run by British settlers. They were paid very little and lived hard lives while the British took the profits. In the late 1950s, a rebellion against British rule took place, known as the Mau Mau Uprising. The rebellion was crushed by 1959, but four years later Kenya gained its independence and the British left.

Far left: The Kenyan national flag. The spears, shield, and colors represent the right of Kenyans to be able to farm in peace.

Left: Children playing in the warm waters of the Indian Ocean, on a Mombasa beach

Today, Kenya is divided into eight provinces, each with many districts and forty different ethnic groups. Agriculture provides most of the jobs, and the food and goods produced are sold for export. Tourism is also very important, and industry is on the increase.

▲ *This book will take you to the city of Mombasa and the village of Matinyani, as well as the rest of Kenya. You can find these places on the map.*

Kenya's soldiers have often served the United Nations. Kenya has friendly relations and good communications with many countries, especially Great Britain. This has allowed Nairobi, the capital, to become an important center for large companies such as Shell Oil.

KENYA FACTS

Population:	**27 million**
Area:	**224,100 sq. mi.**
Capital:	**Nairobi (1.7 million people)**
Currency:	**Kenya Shilling (K Shs)**
Languages:	**National: Kiswahili**
	Official: English
National motto:	*Harambee!*
	("Let us pull together")

Source: *Republic of Kenya (Statistical Abstract, 1990)*

The City of Mombasa

Mombasa is Kenya's second largest city after Nairobi. It is a port and harbor city and is divided into mainland and island Mombasa. The city was founded by the Greeks in the seventh century A.D. It has a long history of wars and conquest, and has always been a major trading center. During British rule in Kenya, Mombasa was such an important port that it was made the country's capital.

Goods pass through the harbor to and from Kenya, Uganda, Rwanda, and other neighboring countries. The city is home to monuments and beaches, and Kenya's national parks are nearby. This makes it a popular destination for tourists. Travelers to Kenya can arrive in Nairobi first or fly directly to Mombasa. There are many different ways to travel between Nairobi and Mombasa, but many people find that the twelve-hour, overnight train journey is an exciting experience.

Looking over Mombasa Island. As the city grows in importance, skyscrapers replace the old office buildings.

MOMBASA FACTS	
Area:	District: 106 sq. mi. Island: 6 sq. mi.
Population:	700,000
Languages:	Kiswahili; Miji Kenda

Source: *Mombasa District Development Plan, 1989*

Unlike many Kenyan towns, Mombasa does not belong to any single ethnic group. Its inhabitants are a mixture of many different peoples, from all over Kenya and the world.

The city also has a mixture of the old and the new. The Old Town is filled with ancient Arabic buildings, and the Old Harbor is often busy with traditional sailing boats, called *dhows*, carrying tourists. In contrast, less than two miles away is the modern Kilindini Harbor, which handles many big cargo ships and oil tankers.

Map labels:

To Nairobi & Mombasa Airport

Makupa Causeway

Kipevu Causeway

New Nyali Bridge

Old Nyali Bridge

Market

Mombasa Harbor

Mombasa Showground

OLD TOWN

Kilindini Harbor

N

MOMBASA CITY

0 — 1 km
0 — 0.5 miles

Legend:
- Major roads
- Railroad
- Industrial areas
- Mosque
- Tourist attractions
- Ferry crossings
- Hospitals

▼ *On the way to the beach, people can buy roasted corn and coconuts from this roadside stand.*

7

The Village of Matinyani

Matinyani is a small village in the Kitui district, southeast of Nairobi. Kitui is one of the two districts of the Akamba people. Homes are simple and are shared by many people.

Most of the men in Matinyani work as farmers or herders. The climate is so dry and water is in such short supply that everyone has to work hard to make a living.

Many of the women in the village take part in projects where they learn to make rugs, baskets, and other handicrafts. They use the fibers of sisal plants that grow around the village. The handicrafts are then sold to shops in Europe.

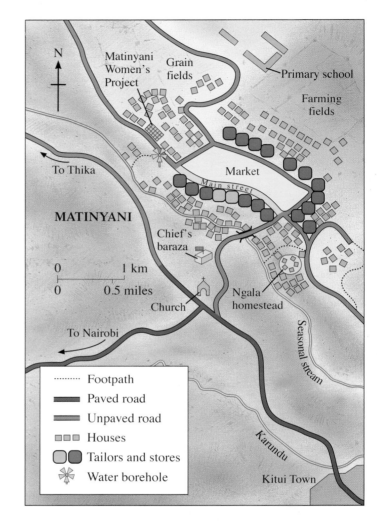

MATINYANI FACTS

Population:	5,000
Number of houses:	500
Languages:	Kamba; Kiswahili

The village hotel and bus stop in the main street of Matinyani

8

Matinyani's main street has a hotel, three butchers' shops, four bars, and several secondhand clothes and tailors' shops. There is also a marketplace, where a market is held every Friday.

Young people often move away from the village to Mombasa or Nairobi when they are older to look for work. The government is trying to make improvements in Matinyani to reduce poverty and encourage people not to leave. Trees are being planted to keep the soil from eroding, roads are being built, and water supplies have been improved.

Women from the Matinyani Women's Weaving Project with a basket they are making. Baskets are made in many different colors, designs, and sizes.

Landscape and Climate

Kenya lies on the equator, so the sun is very hot and shines for twelve hours a day. The rivers are poor for travel, but their water is used to produce electricity, and dams have been built to create reservoirs for fishing and irrigation. From April to June, heavy rains cause serious floods on the shores of Lake Victoria in the west and the Indian Ocean in the east.

The climate in different parts of Kenya is affected by the height of the land and its distance from the sea. The coast is hot and wet all year-round, which is ideal weather for growing coconuts. But the coconut plantations leave little room for other farming. Mangrove swamps and white sandy beaches line the shores.

Picking tea on a plantation in the highlands west of the Rift Valley

KENYA'S LAND AND CLIMATE

Hottest temperature:	above 95° F (deserts)
Coldest temperature:	below 41° F (slopes of Mount Kenya)
Hottest months:	November–February
Coldest months:	July–August
Heavy rains:	April–June
Highest point:	17,060 ft. (Mount Kenya)
Longest river:	435 mi. (Tana River)

Source: *Republic of Kenya (Statistical Abstract, 1991)*

▼ *Tourists on safari in one of Kenya's wildlife parks. Tourism is an important source of income in Kenya.*

▼ *Good roads mean that the fertile central highlands can now be easily reached.*

The north and east sit on a plateau 3,280 ft. high. This means that the rainfall, soil, and vegetation are poor. In these regions, animal herders have to keep moving to find water and fresh pasture for their animals to graze. Although the days are hot, the nights can be very cold.

In the south of Kenya are the grasslands, home to the country's famous wild animals. Here, national parks protect wildlife such as antelope, elephants, giraffes, rhinoceroses, and zebras.

From the grasslands, the land climbs into the highlands, where Kenya's coffee, tea, and flower farming takes place. These "White Highlands" (named after the former European settlers) have a temperate climate. Finally, the Lake Victoria Plateau has good soils and rains, but it is very hot.

Hot and Humid City

▲ *Likoni Ferry takes passengers from the island to the southern mainland of Mombasa.*

Mombasa Island fits neatly into a horse-shoe-shaped creek. A 130-foot-deep channel leads to Kilindini Harbor and a ferry crossing connects the island with mainland Mombasa to the south. To the west is a causeway, and to the north, the two old and new Nyali bridges.

Mombasa's climate is typically humid, hot, and wet, and houses are designed to allow as much air through them as possible. In April and May, there are big downpours of rain. Between October and December there are shorter rains. The climate is good for coconut palms and mangrove trees, which dot the coastline. Tropical fruits, including mangoes, oranges, lemons, and papaws are abundant, some growing wild.

◄ *Camels come from the dry north of Kenya, but some are brought to Mombasa for pleasure rides on the beaches.*

Mombasa Island is mainly a business area, and office space is expensive because of limited space and high demand. This has sometimes meant that new, high-rise office buildings have replaced old historic houses. In the crowded Old Town, the streets are so narrow in places that people on upper floors can reach to one another across the street.

Most wealthy people in Mombasa live on the northern mainland. Tourist hotels stretch along the shoreline, and their private beaches merge into the 130- to 300-foot-wide coral reefs. South of the city there are fishing villages surrounded by small farms.

MOMBASA'S CLIMATE

Average yearly rainfall:	**41 in.**
Average daily temperature:	**77–91° F**

Source: *Mombasa District Development Plan, 1989*

The view across Nyali Creek from the mainland to Mombasa Island

Dry Plateau

Matinyani sits on a dry plateau area, 3,280 feet above sea level. During the wet season, the winds that bring rain from the Indian Ocean bypass this region and take heavy rain to Mount Kenya instead. The heavy water runoff from the mountains causes injury and death to people and animals. It also damages property, crops, trees, and roads. Many projects are under way to restore tree cover to help reduce soil erosion and the loss of rainwater. This would also improve the year-round supply of safe water.

MATINYANI'S CLIMATE	
Average yearly rainfall:	28 in.
Average daily temperature:	61–82° F
Source: *Kitui District Development Plan, 1989*	

A typical roadside goat market near Matinyani. Almost nothing can grow on this dry soil.

▼ *A villager carries homemade brooms to the market. People walk distances of up to 12 miles to get to the market in Matinyani.*

▲ **This land is green after the rains, but the short mango trees show that crops will not grow well there.**

During the dry season, there is so little rain that water shortages and drought are common. Crops wilt, and pastures and dams disappear. Only the sisal plant thrives. People have to travel far to find water, which is carried in containers by people on foot or by using ox-drawn carts.

Without the help of food brought in from outside the village, drought kills many animals and brings famine to the villagers. The climate of flooding and drought is too extreme for farmers to make a living. Much research is being done on seeds that can grow quickly and be used for food under such low rainfall conditions.

Home Life

There are many different ethnic groups and religions in Kenya. Each has its own culture and way of life, but the family is important to all groups.

Kenya's population is growing fast, and the majority of people are under 15 years old. The average Kenyan family has four children. But there are often more than six people in each home, because in rural areas it is common for one man to have two wives, and relatives often live together.

In the countryside, many families live on homesteads with more than one house. The parents, young children, and girls live in the main house, while older boys live in smaller houses on the compound. Grandparents are looked after by their children and grandchildren.

MAJOR ETHNIC GROUPS IN KENYA	
	POPULATION
Gikuyu:	6 million
Abaluhya:	4.5 million
Jo-Luo:	4 million
Akamba:	3.5 million
Kalenjin:	3.5 million
Non-Kenyans:	0.25 million

Source: Adapted from *The Courier*, May–June, 1996

Inside a basic rural home. The radio and the thermos bottles are the only signs of modern life.

▲ *These narrow streets of Mombasa's Old Town have many small apartments.*

Life in the towns and cities is different. Housing is limited, so many people live in overcrowded apartments or houses made from makeshift shelters. In contrast, wealthy Kenyans live in large villas, own many cars, and are waited upon by servants.

Many men leave their village to live and work in a town. To save money, their family will stay in the village, where the children go to school.

Different ethnic groups have their own traditional dishes. Meat, *ugali* (a porridge of corn flour that is boiled until it hardens), beans, and vegetables are eaten most. On the coast, spiced rice, *chapatti*, and fish are common. In the cities, a great variety of foods, including Western and Indian dishes, are eaten.

▲ *Wealthy Kenyans enjoy the luxuries of carpets, electricity, and television in their homes.*

Home Life in Mombasa

Mombasa is dominated by the Swahili and Muslim cultures. Most people live in bungalows with open patios, where families relax and eat their meals in the hot weather.

During festivities, children and adults wear their best clothes.

Saidi comes from a typical Muslim family. He lives with his sister, Fatuma, and their parents on an estate called Majengo. Their home is thatched with palm leaves called *makuti*. The house has a living room, two bedrooms, and a bathroom. At the end of the long corridor there is a cooking area for preparing food. Saidi's house has electricity, but there is no running water. His family has to buy water from a tap connected to a pipe near their house.

Saidi's family eat *ugali* and beans. Fish is also popular, but their favorite food is rice, which is saved for special occasions because it is so expensive.

RAMADAN

During the Muslim holy month of Ramadan, every Muslim fasts from dawn until dusk. At the end of the month, the festival of Id-ul-Fitr celebrates the end of the fasting, and people spill out into the streets at night in carnival mood.

The full variety of food in Mombasa is cooked during the festivals of Id-ul-Nabi (Prophet Muhammed's birthday) and Id-ul-Fitr, which celebrates the end of the Muslim month of fasting.

Every Friday at midday, Muslim men in Mombasa go to pray at one of the mosques in the city. Women are not allowed into the mosques, so they pray at home instead.

▲ *Rich and spicy beef is a favorite festival food in Mombasa.*

When Saidi goes out, he puts on a white, full-length outfit, called a *kanzu*, and a cap. Fatuma wears a black, full-length outfit called a *bui-bui* when she leaves the house.

Saidi and his friends often walk into the wealthy areas of Mombasa. They walk past large houses surrounded by fences and protected by guards. Huge dogs bark at the boys as they pass by.

The boys admire all the expensive cars, and sometimes they glimpse swimming pools and tennis courts at the backs of the houses.

◄ *The rent for apartments like these in Mombasa is cheap, but they are often overcrowded and in poor condition.*

Home Life in Matinyani

Typical village homes with well-trimmed thatched roofs

Ngala and his wife, Mwende, live on a homestead of nine houses in Matinyani. They have three children, aged two, four, and seven. They share the homestead with Ngala's elderly parents, his brothers, and their families. Each main house has earth-brick walls, thatched roofs, and a cement floor. A separate hut acts as a kitchen and storeroom, and there is an outside toilet and bathroom, which is shared by everyone.

Ngala's sisters are married and have moved to their own homes. The younger children sleep in their mothers' houses. As the girls get older, they move to a grandmother's house to be educated into womanhood. The older boys have their own rooms within the homestead.

◀ Mweni Kimanzi, aged seven, eats a bowl of beans beside the kitchen fire. Above her, corn cobs are hung above the fire to dry.

"I will soon pay to have electricity, especially now that I am about to finish building my new, big house."
—Ngala Kimanzi, store manager

Although the nearby market has electricity, not all families can afford the connection fee. So they use paraffin lamps for lighting and cook on open hearths using firewood.

Many people own radios, but very few have televisions. However, some of the bars in the main street have televisions, where villagers can catch up on national and international news. The local chief's *baraza* (meeting place), the Friday market, and Sunday worship are all places for catching up on local news.

Visitors are always made welcome in the village, and they stay wherever there is room for them. Traditionally, it is considered rude for visitors to refuse food that is offered to them.

▲ Donkeys make carrying water faster and lighter work.

21

Kenya at Work

Kenyans are a hard-working people. They have a saying, *kula jasho*, which means "eat from your own sweat." Since there is little paid employment in Kenya, most people work for themselves. In the countryside, many people simply tend their own farms. Others work on the large coffee, tea, or sisal plantations or on cattle ranches.

In the towns and cities, there is employed work in offices or in factories that produce goods to sell abroad. There is also professional work for qualified graduates, such as engineering, medicine, law, and teaching.

But many rely on informal work, known as *jua kali*, where any available scraps are used to make products that can be sold, such as using timber crates to make furniture.

WORKING VISITORS

A popular traditional song says that on the first day a visitor must be waited upon, but by the fourth day they must be given a share of the work to do.

A young girl does her share of the work by herding the donkeys.

▲ *Coconuts are sold at a roadside stand. Work like this is very common in Kenya, where there is little paid employment.*

Since Kenya attracts many tourists, the tourist industry provides different types of work. Hotels near the wildlife parks and along the coast employ people as tour guides, chefs, or general hotel staff. Kenya's two international airports provide jobs as pilots, air stewards, and tour operators. Tourism also provides work to villagers, who sell handicrafts and souvenirs.

Small-scale farmers in the countryside produce enough food for their families and a little extra to sell.

TYPE OF WORK IN KENYA	
	Percentage of population
Small-scale farming:	62%
Informal work:	24%
Employed work:	14%
Source: *National Development Plan, 1994*	

Many women in towns and cities make money by selling crafts and other goods on the street. Younger girls often do paid housework, and many children work after school. Some pupils even leave school to work full-time. Employment for women in towns and cities is usually in catering or secretarial work, but these jobs are only for women who have been to school.

▲ *Construction work is increasing as the demand for new offices rises.*

23

Work in Mombasa

There are many different types of work in Mombasa. Since the city is also a port, there is much work in Kilindini Harbor, where ships bring in goods from other parts of the world. Saidi's father works in the busy warehouses at the shipyard. There is also work in the cement factory, the oil refinery, and smaller factories that make goods such as soap, matches, and corrugated-iron sheets.

Saidi's Uncle Abedi is a taxi driver and owns his own car. He earns good money, but he has to work long hours, so his children see very little of him.

Many people work in tourism in Mombasa, in hotels, nightclubs, or casinos or as tourist guides around the city. These jobs are well paid, and many children leave school early to earn money from tourism.

"I work at the docks unloading goods from cargo ships. We get a two-hour lunch break every day."—Benson Karisa, dock worker

Tourists are taken out on a traditional fishing boat.

▲ **Rajesh Patel helps in his father's office after school. Children start work in family businesses at an early age.**

Saidi's mother is a housewife. She also takes in other people's laundry to earn extra money because Saidi's father's income is not enough. Other mothers do the same, selling snacks or cutting people's hair to add to their family's income.

Fishing is important work to older men in the city, who sell their catch in the markets. But they earn very little money because as the town grows, the fish do not come so close to the shore.

▼ **This boy is increasing his family's income by selling peanuts on the side of the road.**

TYPE OF WORK IN MOMBASA	
	Percentage of workers
Industry	47%
Self-employed	39%
Finance	14%
Source: *Mombasa District Development Plan, 1989*	

Work in Matinyani

▼ *A member of the Matinyani Women's Project weaves a Kiondo basket. The basket will be sold to make money for the villagers.*

There is very little paid employment in Matinyani because there are no businesses there. So many people work in Mombasa, Nairobi, or other towns. They send money home to their families and return briefly for weekends and holidays.

Most people in Matinyani work as farmers growing corn, millet, and beans. They also keep cattle, goats, and donkeys, and everybody in the family shares the workload. A few people work as tailors, shopkeepers, or butchers.

Ngala is lucky to have a job as a store manager for the Matinyani Women's Weaving Project. The project has six people who train women in

▲ *An ox-drawn cart delivers blocks to a building site near the village.*

"In *harambee* (fund-raising) work, everyone must chip in. So for a house, the men will build and the women will make bricks and carry water. The children will gather pebbles and stones, and run errands. In this way the house is really ours!"—Ngala Kimanzi, store manager

handicraft, weaving, and pottery skills. Their colorful rugs and baskets are sold locally and to Europe. Other women's groups keep bees, chickens, and goats.

Ngala's brother grows and sells tree and flower seedlings. These are important to the area because they save water and keep the soil from eroding.

Friday is market day, and men and women bring their cows, goats, and farm produce on ox-carts, donkeys, bicycles, and on their backs. Some people walk long distances of up to 12 miles to get to the market. Afterward, the bars and shops on the main street do a little business before the villagers return to their quiet lives.

Elephants are woven into a colorful rug made by the Matinyani Women's Weaving Project.

Going to School

Although primary education in Kenya is free, secondary school is very expensive. Because of this, many children, especially girls, leave at the end of primary school to work.

Most schools are built through contributions of money and voluntary help from the community. Where there are not enough classrooms, children learn outdoors, or classes take turns using the available rooms. Each child is supposed to wear a school uniform and buy his or her own books, but many families cannot afford these needs.

School is hard work, especially for girls and children from poorer families, who have to do jobs at home as well. At the end of primary and secondary school, students take national exams. To prepare for these exams, they have to go to extra lessons at the weekends and miss their eight-week school holiday.

Fourteen subjects are studied in primary school, including math, Kiswahili, and English (the language in which children are taught). Nine are studied at secondary school. Teachers are trained in the skills needed to teach children with special needs.

Lunchtime in a secondary-school playground in Kenya

SCHOOL IN KENYA	
	Age
Primary school	7–14 years
Secondary school	14–18 years
University	18–22 years

Source: *National Development Plan, 1994*

▶ *The high cost of this nursery school means that the children have access to good equipment.*

Outside the classroom, students can enjoy drama, music, and a variety of sports and after-school courses are popular. Since Kenya has only eight universities, many students leave the country to go to a university abroad.

▼ *Schoolchildren play a game with a homemade ball in their lunch break.*

School in Mombasa

There are many schools in Mombasa, including both state and private schools. Saidi's school is near his home on Mombasa Island, so he can walk home for lunch. Older children, who go to mainland schools, take packed lunches or money to buy snacks.

Most children walk to school, but if they want to catch the bus, their school uniforms allow them student fares. Children from wealthier families are sometimes driven to school.

Saidi is ten years old. He enjoys math and is planning on studying engineering at college. Saidi wants to be able to build a bridge like the Nyali, which crosses Mombasa Harbor.

His sister, Fatuma, is 14 and is studying for her national exams at the end of primary school. Fatuma leaves home for school at 6:00 A.M. to study for 12 hours each day. Fatuma's father wants her to pass her exams so that she can be the first girl in the family to go to secondary school. At least her housework duties have been stopped for the year!

A schoolgirl waits for the school bus, while a matatu *driver tries to attract passengers to ride in his minibus.*

▲ *At the Mombasa district primary schools track meet, runners do their best for their school.*

Sports are important in all Mombasa schools, and annual school competitions are a big event. Sports include swimming, track, soccer, rugby, and netball. Many children learn to swim in the ocean because few schools have swimming pools.

The winners of the 110-meter hurdle race are presented with their prizes.

"I am hoping that if I train hard, I will be able to join the Olympic running team for Kenya in a few years."—Ruth Mutinda, age 14, Kamodya School (above right)

School in Matinyani

Mweni and Kyalo go to Matinyani Primary School, which is about a mile and a half from their home. The rest of the 800 pupils come from up to three miles away. Each class has about 30 students.

Unlike schools in Mombasa, the children do not have to wear shoes and socks as part of their uniform because many parents cannot afford them.

There are no lockers at their school, so Mweni and Kyalo have to carry all their books, as well as their lunch, to school and back each day. They don't mind carrying sports, music, or drama equipment, because the best students travel to other villages and towns for competitions.

▲ *Barefoot on the soccer field. The ball is made out of paper, plastic, and string.*

▲ *The school in Matinyani is neat and simple.*

"I like it when the rains come because we don't have to go so far to carry water."—Mweni Kimanzi, 7 years old

The children of Matinyani Primary School have to keep their school clean. They wash the classrooms and weed the flowerbeds in the school compound. Sometimes they have to do these chores as punishment for being late or for getting into trouble, but they prefer to work rather than to be punished.

During the rains, the children enjoy working on the school farm. It is very different from their home farms and produces much more food. The children enjoy pushing or digging out the vehicles that get stuck in the mud outside the school. The rains also mean that less time is spent carrying water because the tanks and nearby dams are full.

There is no secondary school in Matinyani, so students who pass their national exams have to go to school in Kitui town.

Mweni and her friends looking out of their classroom window

Kenya at Play

Evenings, weekends, and vacations in Kenya are spent on favorite pastimes such as sports, meeting with friends and family, or simply catching up on jobs around the home.

Kenya is famous for producing some of the world's best athletes, especially long-distance runners. Olympic champions are an inspiration to young Kenyans, many of whom have to run long distances to and from school every day and who hope to become Olympic gold medalists themselves one day. Soccer is another popular sport that is played almost everywhere in the country since it does not require expensive equipment.

Other sports and big events are boxing, swimming, tennis, golf, rugby, hockey, horseback riding, cycling, and volleyball. However, only a small percentage of Kenyans have access to these sports because they are expensive and are concentrated in the big towns and cities.

Children play games such as hide-and-seek or hula-hoops and use playthings that usually come from scrap heaps rather than from toy shops.

Children play on a makeshift merry-go-round in a city park.

A traditional Kenyan pastime is a type of fund-raising called *harambee*. This is a way of getting jobs done while also having fun and includes singing, dancing, and feasting. Public holidays are a good excuse for Kenyans to treat themselves and to enjoy time with relatives and friends.

▲ *Soccer is a very popular pastime among Kenyan boys.*

OLYMPIC CHAMPIONS

Since 1968, Kenya's runners have won the 3,000-meter steeplechase in every Olympics and World Cup!

KENYAN PUBLIC HOLIDAYS

January 1:	New Year's Day
March/April:	Good Friday and Easter Monday
May 1:	Labor Day
June 1:	Madaraka Day
October 10:	Moi Day
October 20:	Kenyatta Day (all heroes day)
December 12:	Jamhuri Day (independence day)
December 25–26:	Christmas Day and Boxing Day

The Muslim festival of Id-ul-Fitr is also a public holiday. Its date varies according to the month of Ramadan each year.

◄ *A hurdle race in a match between schools at Mombasa Stadium*

Leisure Time in Mombasa

There are lots of ways to relax and have fun in Mombasa. In the daytime there are beaches for swimmers and sunbathers, and at night there is both modern and more traditional dancing.

Families can visit crocodile farms, meat-roasting dens, called *Nyama Choma*, or ancient monuments such as Fort Jesus. Schoolchildren are often taken on trips to the national parks outside the city, to see the wild elephants, giraffes, and zebras.

Soccer is very popular in the city, as it is all over the country. Kenya's third largest soccer stadium, Mombasa Stadium, attracts many fans and players. Sporting events are often big family occasions, and the annual International Mombasa Marathon is a very colorful event.

> **"I have been saving money so that I can enjoy more of the stands at the Mombasa Show this year."**
> **—Salama Karisa, 10 years old**

Relaxing in the warm sea. On the horizon you can see waves breaking on the coral reef that fringes the coastline.

◄ A Muslim family in its best clothes browses for festival goodies at Id-ul-Fitr.

The annual Muslim festival of Id-ul-Fitr is a special occasion for families. People wear bright, new clothes, and many activities take place on the streets. Other festivities include the Mombasa Agricultural Show, which attracts visitors from all over the country and provides a week of continuous fun for everyone to enjoy. Many Kenyans also flock to Mombasa for their Easter and Christmas vacations.

▼ Giving a friend a lift along the beach

For tourists and wealthier families there is plenty to do. Many go on guided tours into the surrounding national parks. Or they take part in watersports such as water skiing, scuba diving, or deepsea fishing. At night, there are many restaurants to choose from, and the evening breezes draw people to the sea-front gardens.

Leisure Time in Matinyani

Matinyani, like other villages in Kenya, has far fewer leisure facilities than in the towns and cities. So people have to be creative and make their own fun.

Children make toys from local materials such as clay, straw, beans, and sand. They also use cardboard boxes and leftover cloth from the tailors' shops.

Singing is very important in the village because it cheers people up while they work. Since there are no books or comics available to read, singing is a good way of entertaining the children. Many of the songs also teach children about the history of their family or community.

Women hardly ever rest during the day because there is so much work to be done. Instead, they make the most of being with their friends while they work and swap news and stories.

Joseph Kilonzo and his friends with their soccer ball in the street

"We play soccer whenever we get the chance. We've got our own ball and we've marked out a playing field with piles of stones."—Joseph Kilonzo, 14 years old (right)

The men have an easier time because their work, such as herding cattle, means that they can sit and chat together during the day. In the evenings, they go to the local pub and watch television.

The chief of the village is elected by the government and remains chief until he dies. His *baraza* is a good place for the villagers to meet and discuss important matters about Matinyani. The elected leaders also have meetings that often become heated with noisy discussions.

People look forward to the Friday market and Sunday church, when they can wear their best clothes and see their friends. Weddings and funerals are also big events and become occasions for everyone to meet and talk.

▲ *This toy car has been made out of scrap tin, wood, and string.*

▼ *Stallholders sell vegetables and fruit on market day in Matinyani.*

The Future

The future for most Kenyans is in farming, since eight out of ten people in Kenya rely on farming to make a living. However, most farmers have only small areas of poor-quality land, while a few wealthy farmers own huge plantations.

The growth of Kenya's population is adding to this problem. Poor people usually have large families so that their children can help on the farm. But as the number of farmers grows, the quality of the land and produce gets worse. If the government can share more of the high-quality land and if the larger farms can offer work to some of the smaller farmers, people in the countryside would prosper.

Kenya's population is still growing, and all these children will need more jobs and better health care in the future.

POPULATION GROWTH	
	Millions
1989	23.5
1990	24.4
1991	25.3
1992	26.2
1993	27.2

Source: *National Development Plan, 1994*

As the population grows, more young people will be looking for jobs and could face unemployment. As a result, self-employment is being encouraged, especially in the towns and cities.

Kenya's stunning landscapes continue to attract many tourists every year, and the tourist industry should provide more jobs and money in the future. But tourism also causes problems, such as encouraging children to leave school early, that will have to be looked at in the future alongside the industry's growth.

If Kenya can make good use of its large, young population and other natural resources, as well as relying less on other countries for help, Kenyans should be able to feel proud of their independence and successes.

▲ *A guide driving tourists through a wildlife park. He knows the best places to watch the animals.*

▶ *The entrance to a national wildlife park. This kind of tourism is essential to Kenya's future income.*

The Future of Mombasa

These beautiful beaches could be threatened by pollution from the growth of the city.

Mombasa's future must be carefully planned. It is important that the city's growth in industry and population is balanced against pollution, shortage of fresh water, and overcrowding that growth may cause.

The demand for more office space could mean that historic buildings, which can never be replaced, will be torn down. People in Mombasa are also worried that parkland in the city will be lost as land is taken for housing and business. These could all mean that fewer tourists would come to Mombasa. But the city and its people cannot afford to lose the money that is made from tourism.

On the other hand, it is important that the many visitors to Mombasa do not destroy local cultural values. The Muslims do not want their culture to be affected, and the traditions of the original nine peoples of the area, the Miji Kenda, should be respected. For example, it is essential to them that their *kaya*—sacred prayer forests—are not damaged in any way.

"The new office building is beautiful, but it has been built on our soccer field. Where will we play now?"—Hamisi Omar, 10 years old

At present, school test results in Mombasa are among the worst in Kenya. Many children leave school early to take jobs in tourism, and girls often leave school to get married. This is partly because of the need to earn money, but also because of tradition. If children are encouraged to stay at school, they stand a better chance of getting higher paid jobs at the end of their education. This would mean a better quality of life for themselves and their families.

◀ *New, high-rise buildings satisfy the demand for more offices, but overcrowding may create new problems.*

▼*Improving education is one of Mombasa's most important tasks in the future.*

The Future of Matinyani

Despite their hardships, the people of Matinyani are full of hope for the future. They hope that their lives will improve and that financial help will be offered by well-wishers. For example, the heavy floods can cause terrible damage, but with financial help, dams could be built upstream. This would keep the village from flooding and would create a supply of water for irrigation and drinking.

The village is also hopeful that the arrival of electricity nearby will attract new businesses and new jobs. This might bring back the young, who have left to find work in the city. More important, it might stop young people from leaving their friends and families in years to come.

The famous Matinyani rugs will bring much-needed money to the village in the future.

▲ *Tree cover is essential to protect the soil from erosion. If projects to restore tree cover are effective in Matinyani, crops will be more successful.*

It is hoped that the growth of women's projects will mean more money for education and health care in the village. As the groups become stronger, it will be possible to get better prices for their crafts.

As research on new seeds for crops in this dry land continues, it should mean that more money will be made from farming, and there will be more food to go around. More money should make it possible for the villagers to improve their homes. They should be able to pay for electricity to be connected to their homes and to buy other items to make their lives easier.

"The primary school has been built through *harambee*. I hope to become a leader so that I can build a secondary school for Matinyani."—Joseph Kilonzo, 14 years old

▶ *Small businesses, such as this tailor's shop, do not rely on the success of crops, so they are safer than farming in Matinyani.*

45

Glossary

Baraza A central meeting place in a community where members discuss serious matters or simply chat.

Causeway A raised road built over a stretch of water.

Colony A territory or country that is controlled by another country.

Compound A group of houses with shared facilities, such as toilets.

Crops Plants grown on a farm for food.

Dhows Large Arabian wind-driven boats.

Equator An imaginary line around the earth, which is an equal distance from the North and South poles.

Eroding The wearing away of a substance, such as soil.

Ethnic groups Groups of people identified by their language or culture.

Export A country's produce that is sold to other countries.

Harambee A type of fund-raising in Kenya where people contribute work and money to gain a need, such as building a school.

Homestead A house, especially on a farm, and outbuildings.

Humid Air that is full of moisture.

Independence When a colony gains the right to control its own affairs.

Irrigation The artificial watering of the land to grow crops, using channels, sprinklers, or pipes.

Makeshift Temporary.

Makuti The leaves or branches of the coconut tree, used for roofing.

Matatu A type of taxi, usually a minibus. *Matatu* drivers are renowned for overloading and speeding.

Monuments Historic remains, such as buildings or statues.

Paraffin An oil used for fuel.

Plantation An area of land planted with a single crop or type of tree.

Plateau An area of fairly flat land, raised above the surrounding area.

Rent To pay money to live in a house or apartment.

Sisal plant A plant with large, fleshy leaves. The plant has tough fibers that are used to make rope and handicrafts.

Settlers People who move from their original home or country to live elsewhere, often to farm.

Slums Dirt-filled areas in towns where people live in poor, makeshift housing. Usually there is no proper water supply, lighting, or even streets.

Temperate climate A mild climate that is never very hot or very cold.

Ugali A preparation of corn flour that is boiled until it hardens.

Voluntary Actions done from free will rather than from being paid or forced to do them.

Further Information

Books to Read

Burch, Joanne J. *Kenya: Africa's Tamed Wilderness*. New York: Macmillan Children's Group, 1992.

Cremin, J., and C. Regan. *Africa*. Continents. Austin, TX: Raintree Steck-Vaughn, 1997.

Lerner Publications, Department of Geography Staff. *Kenya in Pictures*. Minneapolis, MN: Lerner Publications, 1988.

Murray, Jocelyn. *Africa*. Cultural Atlas for Young People. New York: Facts on File, 1990.

Ng'weno, Fleur. *Kenya*. North Pomfret, VT: Trafalgar, 1992.

Pateman, Robert. *Kenya*. Tarrytown, NY: Marshall Cavendish, 1993.

Useful Addresses

Kenyan Embassy
Washington, D.C. 20008
202-387-6101

Kenyan Tourist Office
424 Madison Avenue
New York, NY 10017
212-486-1300

Picture acknowledgments:
All photographs are by Paul Kenward.
All map artwork is by Hardlines.
Border artwork is by Catherine Davenport.

Index

Page numbers in **bold** refer to photographs.